Hues Of Poetic Essence

Painting emotions with verses

Renuka Srija

BookLeaf Publishing

India | USA | UK

Made with ❤ on the BookLeaf Publishing Platform
www.bookleafpub.in
www.bookleafpub.com

Dedication

"For those who listen to the quiet spaces between words, who find meaning in the unsaid, and who see beauty in silence. May these verses echo within you and remind you that even in stillness, there is a voice waiting to be heard."

Preface

"In these pages, I invite you to explore the unspoken realms of thought and emotion. Each poem is a delicate balance of silence and sound, where words stretch beyond their limits to touch the heart. May this collection speak to the quiet places within us all."

Acknowledgements

"I extend my deepest gratitude to those whose unwavering support has made this journey possible. To my family, friends, and mentors—your encouragement and belief in my voice have been my strength. This book is a reflection of your love, inspiration, and guidance."

1. A Spark that Died

For just a fleeting moment, you were mine,
I held you close, it felt like the stars did shine.
You looked in my eyes, took my hand so tight,
A spark between us, burning so bright.

I hugged you close, though I knew the cost,
I wasn't supposed to get too close, but I was lost.
You held me tight, chasing my fears away,
In your arms, I felt safe, like everything would stay.

I knew the risk, but I still thought you cared,
That maybe, just maybe, you saw me rare.
But you left me stranded, just like the rest,
With only a note and some empty promises to digest.

You loved her for years, yet she turned away,
Left you alone, with nothing to say.
I was angry, not just at being left behind,
But for being treated like I was blind.

I knew the risks, but I felt so alive,
For that moment, I felt like I could thrive.
But I hated myself for being treated so cheap,
When I deserved love so pure and deep.

The guilt inside ate me alive,
For letting you make me feel like I couldn't survive.
I know karma's real, it'll find its way,
And soon, you'll pay for the games you play.

I got my lesson, but so will you,
My curse will rise, and you'll see it too.
For in the end, the love you wanted the most,
Will slip away, just like a ghost.

2. Shattered Heart

I knew I was a second choice, yet still, I couldn't deny,
That all I believed in was a carefully spun lie.
I loved him like a dove, gentle and serene,
He was meant to be my knight, my fairytale dream.

I reassured myself, perhaps I was at fault,
That his intentions were pure, and mine would never
halt.
I would've given everything, my heart laid bare,
For him, I adored with a love so rare.

He told me I was different, unlike those before,
That with me, he felt something more.
A kiss upon my cheek, I blushed with grace,
He said he'd miss me if I left his embrace.

He told me he couldn't sleep, yearning for my time,
I imagined he'd ask for my heart, that moment so
sublime.
I gave him trust, even when it was not deserved,

Hoping one day, his love would be preserved.

But then, he said I no longer mattered at all,
I questioned how, when just yesterday I stood tall.
I grew weary of being deceived, a pawn in his game,
Now I stand broken, with nothing but shame.

I knew I was just a spare, but still, it was hard to see,
That everything I had believed was just a fantasy.
I loved him like a dove, too pure to fight,
He was supposed to be my knight, my fairytale, my light.

3. Unspoken Love Lost

You never truly grasp the love that's concealed,
The one you desire, the one you seek,
We remain unaware of the hearts we sway,
And the ones who resist, who turn away.

You never recognize the love we're worthy of,
They perceive us as bold,
Like a dish served cold,
We wander through time, uncertain whom to choose.

You never notice, or we simply ignore, the love we
receive,
The glances we invite,
But now we see the final regret,
That unspoken wish, that love we never embraced.

You never know, the hidden love,
The one you thrive, the one you crave,
We never know, of the hearts we melt, the one they
resist,

You never know, of the love we deserve,
They think we are bold,
Like the dish served cold,
We never know, by passing day, on whom to date,

You never know, or we Ignore, the love we get,
Of the eyes we set,
But now we know, the last regret, that wish we met

4. Alive in the Shadows

I crave danger, danger craves me,
Endless feasts they lay before me,
Each time it feels like I am crawling back,
From the grave, where only in darkness do I truly live.

Daily routines, wearing the same masks, clutching my
halo,
The same halo, repeating endlessly, day after day,
But as night falls, darkness stirs within, deep and
endless,
That is when it strikes, a danger I cannot resist.

I feel the shadows as I crawl back,
From the grave, the only place I come alive,
The danger consumes me, or do I consume it?
Invisible to the world, yet I have never felt more seen.

I feed on it, devour the danger,
Ripping hearts from chests, leaving nothing but
emptiness,

Hearts I once mended, healed by the light,
But in this madness, the ripping feels so wrong, yet so
right.

I crave danger, danger craves me,
Endless feasts they lay before me,
Each time it feels like I am crawling back,
From the grave, where only in darkness do I truly live.

5. In-between Love and Healing

I want to write, I want to inspire,
But my mind feels numb, my heart still caught in fire.
I'm getting better, day by day,
Trying to forget you, pushing you away.

I just want to write, that's all I seek,
Something about love, something bittersweet,
A tale of healing, a release from the pain,
Of learning to love, and forgetting the strain.

I keep asking myself, who am I writing for?
Nothing reminds me of love anymore.
The stars no longer shine so bright,
And moonlight doesn't spark the same delight.

My heart no longer races, steady and slow,
The curve of my smile doesn't feel like it used to glow.
I'm left with silence, don't know what to say,
But I just miss love, in every way

6. When Stars Collide

He was a man of passion, with charm, but love was far,
She, a vision of grace, the brightest, like a shining star.
Always close, yet never one, forever side by side,
Silent glances, tender smiles, emotions they could not
hide.

It felt as if their hearts were bound, though they stood
worlds apart,
A love so deep, yet out of reach, each holding the
other's heart.
Each day they'd look up to the sky, their love they'd
silently show,
But neither had the strength to speak, to let their true
hearts flow.

She, shy and delicate, would blush in his presence near,
While he, with words unspoken, kept his love locked in
fear.
Still, their souls understood the bond, more than words
could ever say,

A love so pure, so deep, yet trapped, each waiting for
the day.
She, overwhelmed by love's sweet pull, could no longer
keep it inside,
He, at last, had found the courage, no longer willing to
hide.

Together, they promised under the stars, they'd share
their hearts so true,
That on the sacred day they'd meet, their love would
break through.
On that day, she wore the silk, he wore the woven
thread,
Running to each other's arms, their hearts both filled
with dread.
But fate, so cruel, played its hand, a fallen star did strike,
He, caught in its deadly blaze, and she, in the same fight.

Inches from each other's touch, love's promise in their
eyes,
But all they had were falling tears, and unspoken
goodbyes.
On that fateful, destined day, when love should have
been free,
Both lost their lives to fate's cruel game, their souls too
wild to be.
Like Vega and Altair in the sky, together yet apart,

A love that soared beyond the stars, forever in their hearts.

12

7. Love's unwritten song

He's a warrior who never fought, yet every night, he
brought
The bread that fed the ones he loved, no praise, no glory
sought.
He never asked for thanks or fame, just wanted joy to
reign,
His heart, so full of quiet care, as he worked through
every strain.

He never grumbled, never wept, just kept on with his
fight,
A hero in the shadows, still, a beacon in our sight.
The roles he played were never light, ensuring smiles
would stay,
He taught his son to show respect, and led his girls the
way.

He gave his all to his love of life, and built a life anew,
Tended to the hands that gave him life, with a love so
true.

He was told men never share their pain, that they must
stand alone,
But even heroes feel the weight when standing on their
own.

He followed dreams that were long passed, yet never left
behind,
The silent warriors in our lives, whose strength we often
find.
These fathers, our unsung heroes, steady, strong, and
wise,
The ones we love, the ones we trust, yet never truly
realize.

----- Dedicated to my Father

8. The Quiet Strength of Her

She's an angel, fallen from the skies,
With a soul so pure, it lights up our eyes.
Her love so true, her touch so kind,
Like holy water, a blessing refined.

A mother to her child, a lifeline to all,
heart so gold, even God wants to be her favourite son,
Though we rarely speak, her love's always near,
She's our temple, and we hold her dear.

We say we're fine, but wish she would stay,
She knows us better than words can say.
We may not always understand, but it's clear,
Her love speaks to us, especially near.

No matter what we do, it's never enough,
Mother's love is a treasure, gentle yet tough.
The first time we called her "mom," she smiled so bright,
Her love's a tale untold, wrapped in light.

She's an angel, fallen from the skies,
With a soul so pure, it lights up our eyes.
Her love so true, her touch so kind,
Like holy water, forever intertwined.

----- Dedicated to my mom

9. The Road to You

When I found him, my heart skipped a beat,
I packed everything again, thinking our worlds would
meet.
The boy from my dreams, the one I adored,
Wondering if his heart was still mine, as before.
Driving down Boulevard, the city lights so bright,
Hoping to find the love I lost in the night.

I reached the city, my nerves all over the place,
Wearing my lace shirt, hoping to see his face.
Sunglasses on, hiding my tears, trying not to cry,
I texted him, "I'm here, will you meet me tonight?"
Sitting in my car, the silence felt too long,
Then his message came, and I knew I wasn't wrong.

In the dress he loved, I stood there, waiting,
My heart racing, my mind hesitating.
I just wanted to know if love was still real,
If this moment could heal what time made surreal.
He walked up to me, a smile I didn't expect,

And all the pain I'd carried, I couldn't neglect.

We didn't need words, just a hug so tight,
I held him close, everything felt right.
He kissed my forehead, his voice filled with regret,
"I searched for you everywhere, I couldn't forget."
His letters never made it, too much time had passed,
Tears filled my eyes, this love was meant to last.

Finally, together, no more waiting alone,
My heart felt whole, finally coming home.
We found each other, through all the years that went by,
Now we're here, no more goodbyes.
In his arms, I felt safe and free,
We've found our road, just him and me.

10. In Love's Wake

Though I speak to you, I still yearn to be near,
Like before, as your love, your partner so dear.
I don't miss the love, for I know it's still true,
Nor the dates we once had, but I long to see you,
As you cook for us, with hands that knew grace,
A memory I cherish, time cannot erase.

I miss the moments, the memories we made,
The way your eyes would draw me, where words often
fade.
The stolen kisses, the glances we'd share,
The late-night talks, a connection so rare.
I miss the warmth of your hand in mine,
A bond that once felt like it would never decline.

I know it's unfair, yet it's the truth I confess,
In just a few months, you left me to regress.
I wish I could whisper to the girl I once knew,
That the knight she adored, was no longer true,

Without a word, without a fight, You slipped away, out
of sight.

11. In the Company of Queens

In a world of fakes that crowd my space,
There stood two bees, always in the race,
Without these buzzing friends by my side,
My therapy would cost a hefty ride!

One was lively, full of cheer,
The other quiet, yet always near,
Both of them prayed I'd find my mind,
To fix my chaos, a peace to find.

I fear their mischief, their schemes to plot,
If I fall out, they'd sting my spot!
Found them on a forum, friends galore,
Now I can't imagine life before.

The chirpy one's fun, the quiet one's a bore,
We bicker like sisters, oh, what a chore!
One would fight for me, the other would fib,
But together, we'd always outwit the rib.

In a world of fakes, they're my true crew,
They buzz beside me, steady and true,
Without them, therapy's a pricey task,
They're the ones I'd never dare to ask—
But still, they quietly pray for me,
To find my sanity, calm the sea.

I'm half-empty without them, can't you see?
Like fish stranded, gasping at sea!

-------- Dedicated to my soul sisters #RoSh

12. Whispers of Petals

I've witnessed smiles, and I've seen knives,
I've been torn on the ground, soaked and drowned,
I've known every part of life, even rode on a broken
bike,
I shine in the sun, and grow when the rain comes right.

I've seen lovers holding me close, hearts beating as one,
But I've also felt the pain when love was undone.
Petals ripped, withered and dry, while tears filled her
eyes,
Wondering why he didn't try, asking herself the whys.

I've been placed on the grave of a soul resting in peace,
Carrying messages from the heart as others grieve and
cease.
I've been worn in the hair of a girl, a token of love,
And laid before the gods by those in need, praying from
above.

I've seen smiles, and I've seen knives,

Torn apart, soaked, and drowned,
I've lived through each phase of life, on a broken bike,
I shine in the sunlight, and grow when the rain falls
right.

13. Sisters, Always and Forever

We yell and laugh, share stories all the time,
Of who's the favorite child, the one that's prime.
They tell us we're equal, like their two eyes,
Now we bicker over left and right, in our playful ties.

I'd give everything for my little one, no doubt,
She'd do the same for me, even if I'm the older sprout.
She keeps my secrets and comforts me at night,
I can't imagine life without her, I'll always be her
knight.

I try each day to do right, as she looks up to me,
Like I'm her only light, her world, her key.
I plan her future so it's always bright,
I'd protect her from harm, through every fight.

She's still my butterfly, my love never dies,
It grows stronger every day, like endless skies.
I want to give her a world of peace, no fear,

Just joy and laughter, with happiness near.

----- Dedicated to my sister

14. Torn at crossroads

He was my light in the dark, the other my knight,
I was strong in the night, but a princess in daylight.
I was fine on my own, until the night would fall,
Then my skin would ache, needing someone to call.
Someone to protect me, someone to guide,
When emotions get too much, I need someone by my
side.

One gave me warmth like sunshine, easing my pain,
The other lifted me up, like a shield in the rain.
Each one gave me something, both love me so deep,
But is it wrong to feel this way, with my heart in two,
torn to keep?
I'm stuck at a crossroads, unsure of where to go,
One makes me feel safe, the other helps me grow.

I look at the stars and tears start to fall,
A girl from a broken past, longing for love through it
all.

Now two want to give her their hearts, one with a
smile,
The other with tears, going that extra mile.

Stuck at the crossroads, lost and confused,
Do I pick a peaceful farm or a place where pain's
abused?
A life of protection, or a love that's free,
I try to love myself, but my heart disagrees.
It's okay to love them both, said someone wise,
But how do I choose, when my heart just cries?

15. Under the same sky

She was my solace, a warmth like woven lace,
Her head resting gently, her gaze lost in space,
Under the cherry blossoms, painting petals bright,
I called her "Poppy," she called me "Ace" in the light.

From the age of five, I couldn't dream of life alone,
Her smile like melting butter, my heart she'd own,
She never lied, but something was wrong,
A shadow cast over her, where once was strong.

Day by day, my Poppy's glow began to fade,
Her eyes grew dim, her laughter delayed,
Something unseen was eating her inside,
The light in her soul slowly died.
Now, no longer does my Poppy speak,
Her silence tells me she's fading, weak.

The monster inside her grew with silent power,
I never expected this cruel, dark hour,
I begged and pleaded to the heavens above,

"Don't take my flower, my one true love."

Together we'd lived beneath the same sky,
I wished the storms would take me, not her to die,
I wept in the night, kept strong through the day,
For my Poppy, I'd never stray.

Each piece of her soul ripped away,
I called on the stars to keep her from decay,
I tried to heal the brokenness in her heart,
But with each passing day, we drifted apart.

Then one day, my flower fell to the floor,
Her eyes held mine, then sought her mother's door,
She whispered goodbye, and tears filled the air,
I felt my heart shatter, consumed by despair.

As my Poppy drifted, no longer in pain,
Resting forever beneath the sky's rain,
I watched her fade into peaceful sleep,
My heart now shattered, my soul to weep.

16. The art of self-love

Sometimes I feel down, like my dreams won't take
flight,
But I remember the moments when I touched the light.
I'm hard on myself, my inner voice says,
"Take it slow, or you'll keep feeling this way."

I treat myself right on days when I feel low,
With dates and adventures, or places I want to go.
Maybe I cook a meal just the way I crave,
Or pamper myself, do something I never gave.

A cozy movie, popcorn by my side,
Or a good book with bourbon, let the world slide.
I light candles, sing to Taylor's tunes,
Or buy something pretty, just for me, no room for gloom.

I'll take it easy, savor each day I'm given,
Respecting myself, with dreams still living.
Joy will come when I let go of the fight,
One day, my dreams will soar, taking flight.

By thinking of those heights I've once known,
I'll stay hopeful and optimistic, and not alone.

32

17. Awake & Dreaming

I'm awake and aware, stuck in a job I despise,
I look through the window, where the world spins by,
Some are smiling, some are down, just getting by,
Then I see the woman of my dreams, her smile lighting
the sky.

I hold her hand, promising love that's true,
She says, "Chase your dreams, they're waiting for you,"
"I'll stand by your side, even when things aren't right,
What's love, if not patient, and a beacon of light?"

I dream through the night, and find my way,
In my dreams, I'm free, where I can stay,
I follow my heart, and let it lead the way,
Hoping I'll stay on this path, come what may.

I find peace in cooking, serving meals with care,
Doing what makes me happy, with love to share,
I wish I had the courage to take that leap,
But she's there to say, "Don't worry, I'll keep."

Her support is my strength, my heart is at ease,
No matter the risk, with her, I'm at peace.

18. Forever In Your Arms

I look deep in your eyes, full of love and pride,
Hoping you'd never leave, always stay by my side.
I hold your hand tight, like a kid with sweet desire,
I loved you more than anyone, a love that could never
tire.

I wanted you to stay, never let go of me,
To keep me close, forever, like it was meant to be.
Did I cling too much? Was I too afraid?
You could've said goodbye, didn't have to just fade.

If I'd known you'd leave, never to return,
I would've prayed to every angel, for you to not burn.
I'd ask them to take me, just let you stay,
But instead, I watched you struggle, as you faded away.

I bargained with demons, at a cost too high,
"Take my soul, let me live with him before I die."
Give me a few more years, just with my only kin,
I waited as he breathed, with a smile so dim.

He wanted to see me, the first thing when he awoke,
Now time is running out, my soul slowly broke.
The demon's grip tightens, as it steals me away,
But I hold you close, wishing we could stay.

Just a little longer, like this forevermore,
But the clock keeps ticking, as my soul starts to soar.

19. In the Veil of Twilight

I gazed in the mirror, filled with pride,
Confident, believing I could have any heart by my side.
In my youth, I was the beauty they admired,
Surrounded by souls who knew places so dark, so tired.

That night, I donned a lime silk dress, so fine,
A radiant smile, a vision so divine.
Eyes followed my every step, none could look away,
I moved with elegance, a queen of the day.
But then, the darkness came, pulling me deep,
Sucked my soul, as I fell into eternal sleep.

The next morning, I awoke with a burning ache,
My reflection, so different, I knew something was at
stake.
No longer the girl I once used to be,
Now stronger, sharper, with a hunger so free.
The darkness embraced me, it whispered my name,
I smiled, but happiness was never the same.

Now, I dwell in shadows, a predator of night,
That fateful night, I was claimed by the bite.
No longer a human, no longer the same,
I roam forever, consumed by the vampire's flame.

I protect those I love from the eternal dark,
Yet I'm a creature now, leaving only a mark.
They no longer desire me, their warmth fades away,
For I am a vampire, cursed to stay.

But my search begins, to find the one who turned me,
With my love by my side, together we'll be.
We hunt the one who gave me this cursed fate,
And with every strike, my revenge is great.

My love now shares this darkness, his soul entwined,
We rise together, leaving the past behind.
Through the endless night, I love him still,
My heart beats for him, with a power and will.

Together, we conquer the shadows, and destroy the evil's
reign,
Now we live forever, untouched by pain.
Always together, and forever.

20. Heart of Gold, lost

She was the flicker in his soul, a light in endless night,
The only one who mended him yet kept hidden from the
sight.
He smiled at her softly, but never let her near,
Always holding back the love, masking every tear.

She wondered in silence; did she make him cold?
Was she paying for a past love, a story untold?
She loved him deeply, without a sign of regret,
But each moment with him felt more like a threat.

He held her close on that starry night,
A glass of wine, the love pure and bright,
Whispered sweet words, but they didn't stay true,
Left her broken, questioning what she'd been through.

He called her "heart of gold," said no one could compare,
She believed every word, though it was never fair.
He left her alone, stranded, with nothing but dreams,
Her heart in the distance, lost within his schemes.

She had been his light, in the darkness of despair,
She held him together, yet he never seemed to care.

21. The Silent Beast

They called me sunshine, glowing and bright,
A smile so pure, lighting up the night.
Everyone around me, happy and free,
My voice so sweet, a lullaby's decree.

But as night fell, my smile would fade,
I'd bury the heads of those who betrayed.
My floral dress twisted, torn at the seams,
Eyes turning dark, drowning in screams.

By day, I wore the mask of light,
But at night, I released all my might.
I fed on the fear of those who envied my glow,
The darkness inside me, beginning to show.

Bright in the day, but shadows in the night,
Slowly consumed by the darkness's bite.
It's harder now to hide what's inside,
The evil rises while my angels collide.

The ones who loved me, now left unprotected,
As my hidden life becomes reflected.
I was once pure, but now, I'm undone,
In the shadows I thrive, beneath the sun.